ITALY

A Photographic Journey

TEXT: **Rupert Matthews**

CAPTIONS: **Pauline Graham**

DESIGNED BY: **Teddy Hartshorn and Justine Davies**

PHOTOGRAPHY: **Colour Library Books, Telegraph Library**

EDITORIAL: **Jane Adams and Pauline Graham**

PRODUCTION: **Ruth Arthur and David Proffit**

DIRECTOR OF PRODUCTION: **Gerald Hughes**

CLB 2561
© 1991 Colour Library Books Ltd., Godalming, Surrey, England.
This 1991 edition published by Crescent Books,
distributed by Outlet Book Company, Inc., a Random House Company,
225 Park Avenue South, New York, New York 10003.
Printed and bound in Hong Kong

ISBN 0 517 06539 8

8 7 6 5 4 3 2 1

ITALY

A Photographic Journey

Text by
RUPERT MATTHEWS

CRESCENT BOOKS
NEW YORK

The sun shines in Italy as it shines nowhere else on earth. The still heat is heavy with the deafening chirping of crickets and the scents of the flowers and shrubs which carpet the baked earth. By the dusty roadside, in the shade of some ancient arch, a group of locals sip wine. They wave their arms wildly, emphasizing an argument to which none of the others is really listening.

Cut off from the rest of Europe by the soaring Alps, the Italians have developed a culture and character unique to their peninsula. They generally don't respond well to officialdom, and the resultant chaos has caused more than one headache for those intrepid enough to try to govern them. It is thought, for example, that more than half of the Italians who should pay tax, don't – they are not inclined to obey government edicts, and local officials are not too concerned about enforcing them either. Indeed, the national economy is in such a muddle, as far as officialdom is concerned that, while most people are busy and doing rather well, government figures paint a picture of unmitigated gloom. Italians are, of course, a famously stylish people. The splendid uniforms and celebrated quick march of the crack riflemen are well known throughout Italy and excite the admiration of all. The *Carabinieri*, their élite police force, parade in splendid uniforms dating from a previous century, splendid with epaulets, lanyards, cocked hats and colorful plumes. Not only in the army and police force is such style manifested, but also on the streets and in the wine bars. Elegance has become synonymous with Italy.

Despite such common features, Italians are fiercely proud of their local communities. The expression *terra* may refer to any of a number of things, but is often taken to refer to a region. There are still, for example, unmistakable Neapolitans, Sicilians and Milanese folk, all of whom speak their own version of Italian and who, in many cases, resent the fact that theirs was not chosen as the standard. Such regionalism is hardly surprising. Little more than a century ago the Italian peninsula was divided into more than half a dozen independent countries. Moreover, sizeable areas were under the control of Austria. A few centuries earlier the situation was even more confused by a proliferation of proud, independent city states. The powerful, separatist heritage of these earlier kingdoms, duchies and republics can still be traced throughout the country today.

Dissent caused by these national divisions came disastrously to the fore in 1848 when popular revolutions swept through Italy, overthrowing despotic tyrants and ending Austrian domination in northeastern Italy. Troops from Naples, the Papal States and all the various small states joined the regular army of the Kingdom of Piedmont in a combined attack on the Austrians in the north. Before long, however, discipline began to break down and suppressed local jealousies to break out. Neapolitan troops refused to take orders from the Piedmontese generals, as did everyone else. Before long the alliance had collapsed and Austria easily defeated the Italians. It was largely left to the charismatic radical, Garibaldi, and his romantic force of a thousand "Redshirts" to inspire a "pan-Italian" spirit and bring about the eventual unification of Italy.

After the debacle of 1848 it may have seemed that Italy was destined to remain merely the "geographical expression" of what may have been a united nation, as Austrian Prince Metternich put it in 1849. But greater things were afoot and the spirit of *Risorgimento* began to gain ground. Quite what the nature of this "revival" was has been the subject of much debate. Some historians see it as an upper-class movement of educated people, others as a mass movement of the population. Whatever else may be argued,

Risorgimento had enormous effects upon Italian history and may be said to be the fundamental reason for the existence of the unified nation today.

The causes of the *Risorgimento* movement can perhaps be traced back to the occupation of most of Italy by Napoleon during the early part of the nineteenth century. The French brought many liberal ideas into the peninsula, and their policy of unification spurred ideas of nationalism among educated Italians. The reactionary reigns of dukes and kings that had been restored after the defeat of Napoleon in 1815 only intensified unrest, and numerous secret societies sprang up. A series of liberal revolutions in 1831 were even less successful than the later risings of 1848. By 1850 it was accepted that liberal revolts were useless and only the Kingdom of Piedmont held out any hope for the *Risorgimento*. In 1859 Piedmont maneuvered Austria into the role of aggressor and, with French help, defeated her in a series of battles. The following peace brought much of northern Italy into the hands of Piedmont, and the moderate liberals would have been content with this success.

Garibaldi, however, was not content. He appealed to the romantic streak in his countrymen to spur them on for more and gathered together a thousand volunteers whom he dressed in striking red shirts. Garibaldi and his tiny force then invaded Sicily, which he took in just three months with the aid of local rebels. To the consternation of the moderates he then invaded the mainland and forced the King of Naples to flee. Piedmont reacted by invading the Papal States and linking up with Garibaldi, who then handed his conquests over to the King of Piedmont, thereby effectively making him King of Italy. Within ten years Venetia and Rome, with the exception of the Vatican, had been added to the new kingdom and it only wanted the break up of the Austrian Empire, following the First World War, for Italy to take up, approximately, its present boundaries. The *Risorgimento* movement, which had begun so inauspiciously, in the hands of Garibaldi had finally succeeded in uniting a country of peoples once thought to be too disparate to work together.

If the Italians are not generally considered amongst the most organized nations in Europe, their world leadership in the arts has never been questioned. It is not just that they have produced some of the greatest painters and sculptors in history; the whole nation seems to have an innate sense of good taste. Nothing is too ordinary to warrant artistic attention, even the slabs of concrete which pave the footpaths are worked with elegant designs. The uniforms of the troops which failed to defeat the Austrians in 1848 were the most gorgeous and magnificent in the world. If the Austrians did not respect Italian organizational skills, they must have envied those uniforms and their well-documented ability to impress the *signorinas*.

Even a thousand years ago the talent of Italian craftsmen, particularly their armorers, was recognized throughout Europe and their work highly sought after. It was, however, with the Renaissance that Italian artistry began to emerge in all its glory. Known to the Italians themselves as the *rinascimento*, or "rebirth," this age was characterized by great excitement as the learning and culture of the Ancients was rediscovered and adapted to the period. Italy rediscovered the legacy of the Roman Empire. The numerous sculptures and bas-reliefs, which were literally lying around, gave inspiration and precedents to artists eager to create the new style. Those artists were fortunate to be living in Italy at that time. The whole country was split into innumerable city states, each jealous of its independence and proud of its heritage. The rich *signori* were keen to emphasize their power, for the benefit of their own people as well as other rival *signori*. To do this they spent lavishly on palaces and cathedrals which, to this day, remain as tributes to their wealth and taste.

The Renaissance was a comprehensive flowering of cultures and thought. It was during the Renaissance that the madrigal craze swept across Europe, having originated in Italy. It was also at this time that the arch-pragmatist, Machiavelli, codified his political thoughts. It is, however, for the astounding achievements of the visual arts that the Italian Renaissance is best known. Throughout the country beautiful buildings adorned with magnificent sculptures and paintings were going up, gloriously emphasizing this rebirth of the grandeur that was once Rome. When Brunelleschi crowned the cathedral of Florence with a massive dome, the Renaissance had really begun. It was to produce such artists in Italy as Michelangelo, Donatello, Titian, Botticelli, Raphael and Leonardo da Vinci.

Today, however, the most popular contribution of Italian culture to the world is probably *la dolce vita*, their easygoing, indulgent attitude to life. Italian cuisine has long been recognized as ranking among the world's best. As far back as 1860, Mrs Beeton was extolling the values of pasta and declaring that the very best was made in Naples and exported direct to Britain. The emigration of thousands of Italians to many parts of the globe has helped spread knowledge of their cuisine and wines. The style of cooking thought of as typically Italian dates right back to Roman times, and to the introduction of pasta from China. The Italians have mastered the use of cheese in cooking, and made garlic a byword for flavor. Almost all Italian dishes, from spaghetti to pizza, contain these two vital ingredients, mixed in perfect proportion. In a country where there is little grazing land, the use of red meat has always taken second place to that of poultry, veal and fish. The Italians have devised far more light and appetising dishes from these basics than almost any other nation; dishes which seem particularly tasty when sampled beneath the warm, Mediterranean sun.

Italian wine is very good and has a character all its own, which ideally suits the flavors of Italian cooking. It was not for nothing that the Ancient Greeks named Italy *oenotria*, the land of wine. Even today she still produces more wine than any other country in the world, some 1,750 million gallons each year. The art of winemaking, like most arts, has been perfected by Italy, but their produce is systematized in a rather idiosyncratic way. In France, for example, wines are usually named after the region, or even vineyard, from which they come. Italy, however, has no such system and a bottle may carry the name of a district, grape type, local celebrity or even a purely mythical name of no apparent geographical relevance at all. The government has been trying to introduce a more cohesive labeling system to facilitate selections by foreign buyers for sales abroad, but the current confusion looks set to persist for many years.

Though modern archaeology may point to a much earlier date, the Ancient Romans were adamant that their Eternal City was founded by Romulus in 753 BC. This first king led a highly eventful life, which included killing his brother, Remus. After founding the city, Romulus is said to have had a successful military career before his death in 717 BC. He was followed by six legendary kings, the last of whom was such a tyrant that the Romans deposed him and founded the Republic. Under the Republic, Rome embarked upon an expansionist policy which, by 265 BC, gave her virtual control of the Italian peninsula.

At this time the growing territories of Rome ran into the well-established commercial empire of Carthage. This great North African city controlled huge areas of the Mediterranean and was seen as a threat by Rome, which decided to destroy it. In their first clash, in 264 BC, Rome won the upper hand

and took sizeable territories from Carthage. During the second war of 218 to 201 BC, the exploits of Hannibal nearly brought Rome to its knees. In one battle, that of Cannae, Hannibal massacred 80,000 Roman soldiers and threw his enemy into defensive positions. By 211 BC, Hannibal had advanced on Rome itself and, according to legend, hurled his spear at the gates. However, shortly after the Carthaginians began to lose out to the Romans again, and by 201 BC their power was broken. In 149 BC the Romans attacked again and, after a hard-fought, three-year siege, totally destroyed their rival. Of an initial population of a quarter of a million, only 50,000 Carthaginians remained alive to be sold into slavery.

With Carthage destroyed, no other power could stand up to Rome and the way was open for her to build the largest empire ever seen. At its furthest extent, in the second century AD, the Roman Empire stretched from Scotland to Egypt and from the Atlantic to the Caspian. As the capital for such an immense Empire, Rome grew in wealth, population and prestige. The mighty city became crowded with fine monuments as successive emperors strove to outshine their predecessors and to impress the populace with their own invincibility. *Panem et circenses*, or "bread and circuses," Juvenal's prescription for a contented populace, were perhaps not in themselves sufficient to keep the people happy; they had to be continually reminded of the greatness of their city. It was for this purpose that the majestic buildings were erected, many of them surviving to the present day, despite the onslaughts of barbarians and time.

For the Ancient Romans the most important part of their wonderful city was an area of land which, until the sixth century BC, had been a patch of marshy ground. The Forum, where markets, law courts and popular assemblies were held, was enlarged and embellished by Julius Caesar; an example followed by Augustus and the emperors. Magnificent temples and triumphal arches were raised in fine marbles, making the Forum the epitome of Roman grandeur. After the collapse of the Empire the Forum fell into disuse and was gradually destroyed as its buildings became an official quarry for good marble. By the year 1800, forty feet of rubble and refuse covered the Forum, but throughout the last century a series of archaeological projects has brought its original finery to light.

This small area of central Rome is resplendent with shattered pillars and partial entablatures. The great buildings of the emperors are marked out and their stones replaced as far as possible. But it is not just forlorn remnants which fill the Forum. The majestic Arch of Septimus Severus rises seventy feet into the air. The arch was built in AD 203 to celebrate that Emperor's victories over the Parthians. Nearby is another monument to military victory, Trajan's Column. Wound around the 125-foot-tall column is an 800-foot-long frieze of the Emperor's campaigns, an important source of information on Roman military matters. The column was originally topped by a bronze statue of Trajan, whose tomb this was, but in 1588 a representation of Saint Peter replaced it. The best preserved arch in Rome is that of Constantine, which stands to the east of the Forum. Built in AD 312 to commemorate yet another military victory, this arch incorporates much older sculpture and marble.

Of all the surviving monuments of Ancient Rome to be seen in the present city, the most famous and evocative is the Coliseum. Rising 150 feet, the four-storied arena is a stupendous sight with its monumental proportions and grand arcades. The 50,000 spectators which the Coliseum could hold entered by numbered arches and found their seats by climbing the appropriate staircase. The best seats, those nearest the arena, were reserved for the

Emperor, senators and Vestal Virgins. The opening of the amphitheatre in AD 80 was celebrated by games which lasted for a hundred days and involved 5,000 animals and 1,000 gladiators. The greatest games, however, called for the death of some 2,000 gladiators, and condemned men were often thrown to wild animals in the arena. On other occasions the arena would be flooded and war galleys took part in mock naval engagements. The savage games were amongst the most popular in pagan Rome. Although Constantine the Great banned gladiatorial fights in AD 325, they continued well into the fifth century. In the eighteenth century Pope Benedict XIV consecrated the building, erecting a bronze cross there and dedicating it to the memory of the many Christians who had been executed within its walls.

The Coliseum and Forum are both ruined, as indeed are nearly all the relics of Ancient Rome that can be seen today. But one of the finest buildings, the Pantheon, has managed to survive almost intact. Built by Hadrian in about AD 118 on the site of an earlier building, this remarkable structure is roofed by the largest dome built until comparatively modern times. Spanning 142 feet, the dome is open at the top to admit air and light. In AD 609 the pagan temple was converted into a Christian church, to which the structure probably owes its survival.

At the height of its prosperity, during the second century AD, Ancient Rome had a population of over a million people. The Eternal City, however, had overreached itself and soon began a slow decline. The center of power for the Empire shifted from the city which had founded it to the provinces, which provided the majority of its wealth. In 330 the capital was moved to Constantinople and later the Empire was divided into East and West. In 410 the Western Emperor, Honorius, idled in Ravenna while Alaric and his barbaric Visigoths sacked Rome. The Vandals took Rome in 455 and the last Emperor was deposed in 476, by which time the city's population was down to a quarter of its highest level. The long, inspirational and often glorious era of the Roman Empire had come to a violent end.

Misfortune followed misfortune in the succeeding centuries and, by 1360, Rome's population had fallen to just 20,000.

It was the establishment of the papacy in Rome that saved the Eternal City from the slow decay of so many other important cities of antiquity. With the cessation of barbarian invasions and a return of relative stability to Europe, the papacy played a dominant role in converting the heathens. The word Rome continued to hold a certain magic for the kings of early medieval Europe, a fact which no doubt helped the papacy to survive and expand.

A decline in prestige and the vicious rivalry of several Roman families drove Pope Clement V from Rome in 1309. After a stay in Avignon, France, and the traumatic Great Schism, the papacy eventually returned to Rome in 1420 in the shape of Martin V and embarked upon a course of reconstruction which gained momentum with the years and was to change the face of the Eternal City. The government of the city and the Papal States was reorganized along Renaissance lines and prosperity followed. The dirty, narrow streets of the medieval city were replaced by wide, impressive thoroughfares; and the crumbling medieval structures replaced by magnificent Renaissance buildings. Even the ruthless sack of Rome in 1527 by the troops of the Holy Roman Emperor failed to check its artistic revival. By the mid-seventeenth century Rome was once again a prosperous and majestic city with a population of over 100,000. It is to this period, before corruption and decline once more set in, that the truly great splendors of Rome belong.

St. Peter's Basilica is possibly the most famous building in the tiny sovereign state of the Vatican. The first magnificently adorned basilica on the site of Saint Peter's tomb was begun around 330 by the Emperor Constantine the Great. A thousand years later, however, the building was in such a state of disrepair that in 1506 Julius II ordered a new church to be built. The project took more than a century to complete and the design was changed several times under a succession of architects. The popes involved in the construction were determined that this church should be the finest in the world, and employed such men as Bramante, Raphael, Peruzzi, Michelangelo, Maderno and Bernini to ensure that it was.

Today the Basilica is approached across the thousand-foot-long Saint Peter's Square, designed by Bernini after the church was completed. Its 370 columns and pillars, and the 140 statues of saints make this one of the most imposing approaches in Rome, set off magnificently by the Baroque façade of the Basilica itself. The east front was added by Maderno and was one of the last parts of the church to be built. It was also Maderno who altered the ground plan of the Basilica from Michelangelo's Greek cross to a Latin cross, giving it one arm longer than the other three. Michelangelo's dome, to many the crowning architectural glory of the church, was also altered during construction and is slightly taller than he originally planned.

Quite apart from its architectural value, the church contains some of the finest works of art in the world. The sheer size of the interior is in itself staggering, but the excellence of its detail takes ones breath away. Just within the door stands the *Pietà* created by Michelangelo in 1499, when he was just twenty-five years old. Further into the cavernous interior is found the fine bronze statue of Saint Peter, which is dressed once a year in its jewelled, regal finery. The statue came from the old basilica and probably dates back to the thirteenth century. Over the years pilgrims have continually rubbed and kissed the statue's right foot, to such an extent that it has almost worn away. At the center of the church stands the Papal Altar, which is covered by the magnificent bronze *baldacchino* with its gilded, spiral columns. Scattered throughout the Basilica are the splendid tombs of several popes of the Renaissance and Baroque eras. Perhaps the finest of these monuments are those to Paul III, Urban VIII and Innocent VIII.

Beneath the floor of the present church is the *Sacre Grotte Vaticane*, or crypt, on the level of the original basilica floor. In the the crypt are many more papal tombs, including those of the most recent popes. Beneath this level latter-day excavations of the *Necropoli Precostantiniana* have unearthed the tomb of Saint Peter.

Tucked away within the Vatican is the domestic chapel of the Pope, the Sistine Chapel. Though far smaller than the Basilica, the chapel, with its glorious frescoes, represents the epitome of Renaissance artistry. Those along the side walls were begun as soon as the building was completed in 1481, and were executed by the greatest artists of the day: Botticelli, Perugino and Ghirlandaio. It was almost thirty years before the ceiling was painted by Michelangelo. Depicting scenes from the Creation and Fall of Man, this ranks amongst the master's greatest works. Twenty years later Michelangelo returned to the Sistine Chapel and painted his stupendous *Last Judgement* on the altar wall, a project which took nearly eight years to complete. This magnificent chapel is where the Sacred College of Cardinals are closeted, sealed in, until they elect a new pope.

Despite the glories of the Renaissance, it took many years for Rome to regain its former size. As recently as 1870, Rome still supported fewer inhabitants than were living there when the last Emperor was deposed. In that same year, however, troops of the King of Italy burst through the 1,600-year-old walls to turn the ancient city into the capital of Italy. The population grew rapidly and is now approximately three million, spreading the city out across an area of over 582 square miles. Vast, new building programs and monuments have transformed Rome into a truly modern city. It is primarily an administrative center, and thrives on tourism. No really heavy industry or large-scale commercial establishments are based here. Apart from tourism, this beautiful city of churches, monuments and fountains depends for its livelihood upon its position as capital of Italy and inheritor of Ancient splendor.

Spread across Sardinia, the second largest island in the Mediterranean, are reminders of a unique culture, older even than that of Rome. Huge blocks of basalt stand in large, truncated cones, known as *nuraghi*, which may have been fortresses, watchtowers or tombs. Thousands of them remain and they are almost always within sight of another. The Nuraghese were well known in the Ancient World for attacking their enemies with stone balls.

The Sards have their own language still, despite having been conquered throughout their history by Phoenicians, Carthaginians, Romans, Vandals, Byzantines, Saracens and Italians. Despite this, the island preserved its unique atmosphere and remains as culturally distinct from the mainland as it is politically united to it. The island has its own way of life, language and cuisine – among the native dishes being, of course, the famous pasta dish *malloreddus* and the baked *zuppa cuata*. It is also famous for the vendetta.

Sardinia has always been poor, with meager soil and few natural resources. Moreover, it was continuously plagued by rampant malaria. Sardinia's peasant economy has continued almost unaltered for centuries: cattle and goats are allowed to roam the hills freely, while sheep are herded to protect them from the foxes of the island, and along the coast a thriving fishing industry has long bolstered the economy. More recently the *Cassa per il Mezzogiorno*, a government fund for the development of the impoverished south, has helped Sardinia considerably: after the Second World War, for example, malaria was eradicated by exterminating the mosquito which spread the disease; chemical works have been developed at Porto Torres and Sarroch, and a coal mine sunk at Carbonia. A recently established business consortium owned by the Aga Khan has taken advantage of the disappearance of malaria to develop a holiday resort at Arzachena – a lead followed by others.

Besides its beautiful beaches and wonderful climate, Sardinia has much of interest to offer. As well as the Nuraghic ruins there are many fine churches, some of the best of which were built by the Pisans when they were in control of the island. Saccargia di Santa Trinita, near Sassari, is typical of this type. Of course, it is not only the architecture that is worth seeing, the local people of Oristano and Dorgali daily wear their colorful, traditional costumes. However, it is, perhaps, the capital of the island which best reflects the story of Sardinia. The site of Cagliari was inhabited in prehistoric times, but it was the Phoenicians who founded a city there. For the Carthaginians, during their occupation – succeeded by that of Rome, Cagliari was the principal stronghold. After the collapse of the Roman Empire the city was independent for many years until it came under the control of Pisa, and subsequently Piedmont and Italy. The Pisans left three fine monuments of their overlordship: the Cathedral of Santa Cecilia and the two defensive towers of San Pancrazio and Elefante. The harbor of the town has been enlarged this century and now handles major exports of lead, salt and zinc.

Sicily is in many ways similar to Sardinia, but in many other ways quite different. It is a land still dominated by a somewhat inefficient agriculture. The coastal land is rich, and modern methods of intensive vegetable and fruit growing are now helping to realize its full potential. It is for wine, however, that the island is principally known. Though little of the output is good enough to warrant vintages, it is prolific. The peculiar perfume of orange blossom which pervades the wine makes it indispensable for many dishes, especially the exquisite *vitello alla Marsala*. In addition to the evolving agriculture of the island, the *Cassa per il Mezzogiorno* has helped to attract industry to the island, particularly petrochemical companies based around Gela and Syracuse.

Perhaps the most dramatic feature of the island is Mount Etna, the tallest active volcano in Europe, which stands at the eastern end of the island. This unpredictable mountain rises to over 10,000 feet and was known to the Ancient Greeks as *Aitne*, "I burn," from which its modern name derives. The Ancient Greeks believed that the mountain was the workshop of Hephaestus, the smith of the gods. The most violent eruption in historical times was in 1669, when nearly one hundred million cubic yards of lava were ejected and a dozen villages destroyed. Eruptions have continued spasmodically, with twelve so far this century alone.

The Greeks did not just name Etna, they established important colonies upon the island. Some of the most important Greek remains to be found on the island are at Agrigento, near the south coast. Founded in the early sixth century BC, the city was ruled for a time by the tyrant Phalaris, who is best known for roasting men alive in a large brass bull. After being sacked in turn by the Romans and Carthaginians, the town became part of the Roman Empire in 210 BC. The site was deserted at the fall of the Roman Empire but many buildings have survived. There were originally seven temples on the site, all of which have survived in some form or another. The temples of Hera and Concordia are the best preserved; the latter, lacking only the roof, is one of the most complete Doric temples in the world.

The capital of Sicily, Palermo, is at once Sicilian and cosmopolitan in character. The city was founded by the Phoenicians in the eighth century BC and flourished under later Carthaginian control. Under a succession of rulers – including Romans, Vandals, Byzantines and Arabs – the town languished until it reached its "Golden Age" under the Normans in the twelfth century. During this period its magnificent, domed cathedral was begun, together with the churches of San Giovanni degli Eremiti and Martorana and several splendid palaces. In the later Middle Ages Sicily slipped into decline once again and was always jealous of being controlled from Naples.

The Sicilians eagerly supported Garibaldi when he arrived in 1860, and nearly a century later they achieved autonomous government within the Republic of Italy. Since 1950, moreover, the population of Palermo has leapt from 150,000 to 600,000 as new industry and port facilities have brought fresh prosperity to the region.

After the turn of the first millennium AD, Norman adventurers began arriving in southern Italy. South of Rome, they found that the peninsula was divided up into numerous small, warring states. It was not long before the Normans found an outlet for their genius at war and began to seize lands. By 1130, the "foot" of Italy – or all the land lying south of Formia – and the island of Sicily had been welded into one centrally organized state under Count Roger II. As King of Sicily, Count Roger formed his new domains into a powerful kingdom which would survive changes of dynasty, periods of misrule and foreign invasion for 720 years.

The "toe" of Italy, which separates the Tyrrhenian and Ionian seas, is occupied by the region of Calabria. Despite help from the central government,

Calabria continues to rely upon agriculture for its prosperity. Its traditional staple commodities – olives, cereals, sheep and goats – are now being replaced by cash crops, such as citrus fruits, figs and chestnuts. The wine of the region, however, has continued unchanged; the exceptionally heady red Ciro and the dry white Greco di Gerace being among the most popular. It was in Calabria that Alaric, the chief of the Visigoths, died just a few months after sacking Rome in AD 410. His followers held him in such esteem that they buried him in the riverbed of the Busento, near Cosenza, so that his tomb could never be disturbed. It has never been found.

The "heel" of the nation, Puglia, is in many ways similar to the "toe." Indeed, the Ancients originally called Puglia Calabria. Both are rocky peninsulas which rely on agriculture for their income. In Puglia the strongest wines in the country are produced – they are generally used for blending purposes – as well as other crops also common to Calabria and, indeed, the whole of the Mezzogiorno.

At the heart of the region of Campania stands Naples, the city which took over from Palermo as the capital of southern Italy. This great city was founded around 600 BC by the Greeks. They called it Neapolis, the new town. Its Greek manners and way of life attracted the Romans in droves, and the city became a favorite of several Roman emperors. Their palaces and homes adorned the area and it was here that Nero first performed on stage.

The Roman Naples has long since disappeared, but a glimpse of its erstwhile splendor can be caught twelve miles southeast of the city at Pompeii. By AD 79, Pompeii was a prosperous provincial city with a population of some 20,000 people. Seventeen years earlier, in AD 62, it had suffered a major earthquake and rebuilding work was still under way seventeen years later when nature again took a hand. In AD 79 a tremendous explosion tore through Mount Vesuvius, and Pompeii was buried beneath twenty feet of pumice and ash. The town remained buried until 1869, when excavations were begun which continue to this day. Some three quarters of the city are now laid bare, including some of its finest buildings. Fronting its forum, or principal square, is the Temple of Apollo, complete with forty-eight Ionic columns. Near it stands the fine Basilica. Two theatres and an amphitheatre which could seat 20,000 spectators have also been uncovered. Perhaps Pompeii's greatest value to historians, however, probably lies in its catalog of everyday domestic detail. Dozens of houses, from mansions to hovels, stand as they were all those years ago – as if petrified in the eruption. From this point of view the nearby town of Herculaneum is probably even better preserved. This small town was engulfed by mud to a depth of nearly one hundred feet, which ensured even the survival of wooden artifacts. The wealthier Herculaneum contained finer houses than Pompeii, many with three storeys, and the furniture and statues found in the town are similarly splendid.

The Bay of Naples, which stretches from the Isle of Ischia to the Isle of Capri, is one of the most beautiful in the world with its sparkling waters, islands, shore with green hills and huddled towns – all overlooked by the dramatic proportions of Mount Vesuvius. To the north of the bay is the Isle of Ischia, which covers eighteen square miles. Known principally for its wine, Epomeo, Ischia is rapidly becoming a popular enough holiday resort to rival its famous southern counterpart, Capri. Capri was patronized by the Emperor Tiberius as a pleasure resort. He built a dozen villas here and refused to return to Rome even when he was dying. Today, despite the crowds of tourists, Capri retains its magic. The famed Blue Grotto is a sea cave on the north shore of the island which, particularly in the morning, is suffused with an unearthly light. This strange effect is caused by bright sunlight diffusing into the cave through the water, which covers most of its mouth.

Naples itself has long been recognized as a unique city. Its narrow, winding, steep streets are used almost as living-rooms by the thousands of citizens. After centuries of overcrowding, the Neapolitan way of life has adapted to make a blessing of what elsewhere would be a curse. Poverty has also been endured for centuries and the Neapolitans have learnt to cope with that too.

Despite the poverty, Naples has long been a great cultural center. Through the fourteenth to sixteenth centuries Naples was the unofficial artistic capital of Italy. This phase is reflected in the exhibits of the Capodimonte Gallery, which houses works by Botticelli, Titian, Bellini and Raphael, among others. The architecture of the city also speaks of its past prosperity and grandeur. The Cathedral of San Gennarno at Olmo is a fine structure dating back to 1300, though the site on which it stands was originally that of a temple to Caesar. The Castel Nuovo was first built in 1279, but was rebuilt during the fifteenth century, when the magnificent marble arch was added. The castle grounds adjoin the Palazzo Reale, a seventeenth-century palace of the kings of Naples, which contains some government offices and magnificent state apartments. The palace fronts onto the Piazza del Plebiscito where a fine, semicircular colonnade was erected by Murat, one of Napoleon's generals who received the Kingdom of Naples in 1808. The colonnade is interrupted by the Church of San Francesco di Paola, built by Ferdinand I when he regained his Kingdom after Murat was shot. All along the Via San Biagio dei Librai are run-down, typically Neapolitan palaces. The National Museum contains many sculptures, bronzes and paintings dating from the Roman era, with some particularly fine examples from Pompeii and Herculaneum.

The long history of unity in southern Italy was not the case in the more prosperous north. During the tenth century the Kingdom of Italy, which reached as far south as the Volturno, was ruled directly by the Holy Roman Emperor. As the years passed the Emperor's hold over northern Italy began to slip. The center of Imperial power was in Germany, and local nobles and cities in Italy gained increasing powers throughout the eleventh and twelfth centuries. A long and bitter struggle was taking place between the popes and the emperors as they fought for dominance over each other. The rising families and communes in Italy were able to take advantage of the confusion to increase their own powers. By 1176 Milan was able to defeat an imperial army at Legnano. One hundred years later the Holy Roman Emperor's authority in northern Italy had virtually ceased.

Release from Imperial control came in fits and starts, and each individual city or area achieved its own independence, which it then guarded fiercely. The city states also fought long and bitter wars with each other over boundaries and commerce, resulting in long-standing, deep-seated dislikes of each other. Moreover, within the cities, powerful families struggled for overall control while the ordinary citizens, or *popolo*, tried to wrest power for themselves. These power struggles were made more murderous by blood feud, or vendetta, which, together with intrigue, became a way of life. Despite this, the banking, commercial and trading interests of the states ensured their prosperity and survival. It was against such a background that the Renaissance arose. Each city and every faction turned to art to emphasize its prosperity and power. It is usually for this reason that the cities of northern Italy, many of which are tiny by modern standards, are so resplendent with architectural and artistic treasures.

Urbino is situated in the hills on the eastern slopes of the Apennines. Today it is a rather quiet university town, but five hundred years ago it was a bustling center of art and literature under its ruler Frederico da Montefeltro. The pride of Urbino is undoubtedly the Ducal Palace with its beautiful fifteenth-century architecture and fine art collections. In 1483 Raphael was born in Urbino. Soon afterwards the famous *Urbino maiolica* style of pottery began to be made. In 1626 the Duchy of which Urbino was the center was taken over by the pope, and the city's importance waned.

On the other side of the Apennines stands the town of Siena. Like Urbino, Siena lost its independence to a more powerful neighbor but, unlike the former, it has retained its importance and is now a provincial capital. As the Roman town of Sena Julia, Siena was unimportant, but after freeing itself from Imperial control in 1115 the city gained in prosperity. Its wealth was mainly generated by merchants and bankers who did business as far afield as London and Champagne. In 1260 Siena's army smashed that of Florence at Montaperti, bringing Siena to its peak of power. Unfortunately, Black Death struck the city in 1348, killing half of the 50,000 citizens. Thereafter the rising fortunes of Florence eclipsed those of Siena. In 1555 Siena fell to the Spanish, but not without an heroic defence, and the city was then given to Florence.

During its independent existence, Siena embellished itself with many beautiful buildings which remain to this day. For example, the Cathedral's striking façade of red, black and white marble dates from 1380. The Cathedral itself was begun in 1229, but in 1339 a major rebuilding program was decided upon, intended to make it the largest in Italy. The aforementioned Black Death ended such plans, however, and the Cathedral was never properly finished. The crenellated town hall, which fronts onto the Piazza del Campo, was completed in 1309, though the tower, which is its principal feature, was not finished until the year after the outbreak of Black Death.

The famous Palio race is held in the Piazza del Campo: each year the citizens of seventeen districts of the old city, dressed in medieval costume, join a parade and each district fields a horse in a race around the piazza. The parade is ablaze with the colors of bright uniforms and silk banners. Exhibiting all the grace and beauty of Italian design, the spectacular column of citizens winds through the streets accompanied by flag wavers who hurl streaming banners through the air. The district whose horse wins the race is awarded a *palio*, or banner, emblazoned with the Madonna.

The city state to which Siena lost its independence in the sixteenth century is one of the greatest of Italian cities. Attaining its freedom at the same time as Siena, Florence was then ruled by its merchant families, the most important being the Medici. The Medici originated as peasants in the village of Cafaggiolo, north of Florence. During the twelfth century the family moved to Florence and, by the end of the thirteenth, they ranked amongst the most important in the city. By skilful banking and money changing the Medici increased their wealth to fantastic proportions. Then they turned to politics. After many years of maneuvering, which resulted in execution, imprisonment and exile for various members of the family, Cosimo eventually bribed and tricked his way into power. Using his money and influence, Cosimo established undisputed power for himself without recourse to a title. The succession of power passed to his son Piero in 1464 and then to his grandson Lorenzo in 1469. Lorenzo, named the Magnificent, brought the Medici rule to its height of splendor. The Medici had always associated themselves with the people and with the arts. He lavished unbelievable amounts of money upon architecture, painting and sculpture, making Florence the finest city in Italy. By Lorenzo's time the Medici family was firmly established in Florence, though political errors led to two brief exiles from power. In 1532 Alessandro Medici accepted a ducal crown, a move his ancestors had long avoided, and in 1569 a cadet branch of the family received the title of Grand Duke of Tuscany from the Pope. It was against the background of Florentine political intrigue that Niccolò Machiavelli wrote his classic work *The Prince*.

As the center of an expanding country, and with a ruling house intent upon displaying its wealth and power, Florence was bound to attract artists. Today the city contains a collection of treasures which mark it out from any other city. Yet Florence is not a lifeless museum; there are prospering industrial areas and the city has a population of half a million. Of course, the indigenous population is swamped by the 1,700,000 visitors who come to the city each year to explore the grandeur of Florence's past.

The great museum of Florence is without doubt the Uffizi. Francesco Medici had the palace built in 1560-74 for the efficient band of civil servants by whom he ruled Florence. He also began the collection of great paintings for which the palace is now famous. The Uffizi contains an almost complete record of Florentine painting, including some of the world's greatest masterpieces.

The Ponte Vecchio is, as its name suggests, the oldest bridge in the city and is lined with shops which jut precariously over the river. It dates back to 1345 and was the only bridge across the Arno to survive the Second World War. The nearby Cathedral is the result of a mixture of styles dating from 1296, when it was begun, down to the last century. Its octagonal dome, which dominates the city, was built by Brunelleschi between 1420 and 1436 and is considered by many to be his masterpiece. The center of the old city, however, is the Piazza della Signoria on which stands the Palazzo Vecchio, with its austere façade and fine sculptures. Florence was one of the most powerful of the city states and remains one of the greatest Italian cities.

The third of the famous trio of Tuscan cities is Pisa, now an elegant, provincial city which retains its financial independence through light industry. But during the eleventh century Pisa was a bold and ruthless power. Her fleet was one of the most powerful in the Mediterranean and scored many victories over rival powers. However, in 1284 the Pisan fleet suffered a decisive defeat at the hands of Genoa and two centuries of trading dominance were at an end. So the Pisans turned to industry, and an efficient wool trade tripled Pisa's population to 50,000 in just thirty years. The city then suffered a series of misfortunes: her harbor silted up, internal disputes became even more murderous and divisive than usual and, in 1348, the Black Death struck. By 1406 Pisa was so weak that she could not resist her larger neighbor and the city became subject to Florence. The town's prosperity recovered for a while under Florentine control but soon declined again and, by 1550, the population was down to just 9,000.

The great tourist draw of the city is its famous Leaning Tower, but this is just part of the Piazza del Duomo. Within the Piazza are three beautiful, white marble buildings dating from Pisa's great days. The Cathedral is the largest and was built after a spectacular naval victory over the Saracens in 1063. The circular Baptistry was begun a century later, and took 125 years to build. The Leaning Tower itself was the last of the trio to be built. A slight landslip during construction caused the famous lean, which is at present just over fifteen feet out of plumb and tilts further each year. It was from the leaning tower that Pisa's most famous son, Galileo, is said to have dropped weights to prove that they fell at the same speed.

Tuscany has not only cities to offer, the cuisine of the region is known throughout Italy. Minestrone originated here, as did *funghi alla Fiorentina*, and the Florentines also have a special way with steak. The countryside around the towns is particularly known for its Chianti wines, which may be either red or white and are among the best in the country.

Of all the city states that existed in Italy during the Renaissance only one has remained independent to the present day. The mountainous Republic of San Marino originated in AD 301, when Saint Marinus fled here to escape persecution. It gained its constitution in 1263 and is, therefore, the oldest as well as the smallest republic in the world. The country covers only twenty-three square miles and has a population of 19,000. It was probably because the country is so small and showed no inclination to expand that successive invaders, and the Italian Republic, have ignored it. San Marino has no natural resources. Light industry (using imported materials) is the most important supplier of jobs, followed by tourism, commerce and agriculture. The whole country is dominated by the bulk of Monte Titano with its three peaks. Each peak is topped by a medieval fortress which can be seen from many miles distant.

Of all the great Italian cities only Venice owes nothing to the Roman Empire. When Attila the Hun launched his great offensive into Italy in AD 452, having already devastated vast areas of Europe, one of the cities he destroyed was Aquileia. The citizens of this city, together with the coastal people of Venetia, sought safety on a group of islands in a lagoon. The town they founded became independent of Byzantium during the eighth century and found itself presented with fantastic prospects a century later. The whole situation in the Mediterranean had changed since the fall of Rome. The split between the Pope and the Eastern Church, the rise of the Arabs and the disruption of sea trade placed Venice in a unique position to exploit the riches of the Mediterranean. Galleys from Venice plied the sea, carrying the rich luxuries of the East to Europe, and the grain and gold of Europe to the East. In 1380 the Venetian fleet smashed that of Genoa (which had earlier defeated Pisa) and established a trade monopoly over the area that was to last for centuries.

During those years, Venice became the finest and most prosperous city in Italy, embellishing itself with many beautiful buildings. The city was ruled by a doge, a kind of elected duke, who was advised by the city's nobles. Each year the doge would row out into the lagoon in his fabulous state barge and symbolically marry the city to the sea by casting a gold ring into the waters. At the very height of her power, when the arts were flourishing as never before, two decisive blows were delivered to Venice: Vasco da Gama discovered a sea route to India (1497-99), and Christopher Columbus discovered America in 1492. Venice's position at the center of world trade was lost and, by 1797, she had lost her independence and became subject to other powers.

The city, built on water, may be slowly sinking into the lagoon and the floodwaters may rise higher every year, but it still maintains its beauties and attractions in an atmosphere that is unique. Though the city has recently been linked to the mainland by both road and rail it is still essentially a canal city. Many of the canals, which follow the outlines of the original islands, are so narrow that even gondolas have difficulty in negotiating them. The Grand Canal, however, stands apart. It is never less than 120 feet wide and sweeps in broad curves through the city, lined by 200 palaces and ten churches.

The greatest palace and church, however, are beyond the end of the Grand Canal. Saint Mark's Basilica exemplifies the way in which Venice adapted the various styles to suit itself rather than merely adopting them. It was begun in AD 830, rebuilt in 976 and restyled along Byzantine lines two centuries later. Saint Mark became the city's patron saint in 829 when, under suspicious circumstances, his body, either recovered or stolen, was brought from Alexandria. The fine Campanile was built in 1905, after the original collapsed. The Doge's Palace is said to have stood on the Piazza San Marco, beside the church, since 814, though the oldest remaining section dates only to 1309.

Venice is splendid with evidence of past glories and past prosperity. Modern wealth is the hallmark of two cities to the west: Milan and Turin. The latter was the capital of the Kingdom of Piedmont and was therefore the center for the *Risorgimento* after the defeats of 1848. After Italian unification the city served as the national capital from 1861 to 1865, but it has a much longer history than that. When Hannibal crossed the Alps he found a settlement of the Celtic Taurini tribe in the area, which he destroyed. The site was later converted into a Roman military colony under the name of Augusta Taurinorum, which eventually became known as Turin. After the fall of Rome, Turin lagged behind the great cities of Italy in developing a power base, only coming to the fore after 1418. In that year the city passed into the main branch of the House of Savoy. Since the fifteenth and, more particularly, the seventeenth century, Turin gained in importance as the star of the House of Savoy shone brighter.

The city is today one of the major industrial centers of the nation and has a population of well over a million people. The economy of this thriving city rests on the great Fiat and Lancia works, aero-industries and ball-bearing production as well as a whole host of chemical, electrical and other light industries. Turin does, however, have its aesthetic attractions. The Palazzo Madama, the Royal Palace and the Church of San Lorenzo are fine examples of the peculiar and beautiful form the Baroque took in Piedmont. The Church of San Lorenzo is topped by an unusual dome which dominates the skyline of the city. The Cathedral of Saint John, or Duomo San Giovanni, is faced with gleaming white marble which dates back five centuries. Behind the façade, black marble staircases lead to the Chapel of the Holy Shroud. The shroud is claimed to be that in which Jesus' body was wrapped after His Crucifixion.

Milan lies at the southern entrance to important trans-Alpine passes and, unlike Turin, has long been an important city. Around 600 BC the Gauls settled on the site and, by the time the Romans took over in 222 BC, Mediolanum, as it was called, was an important town. For a while the city became the administrative center of the Western Empire, but in 452 Attila the Hun sacked the city, and in 539 the Goths completed the work. During the early Middle Ages the city prospered and, after a bitter war, broke free of the Holy Roman Empire. The thirteenth century saw a struggle between rival factions within the growing city, which resulted in the dominance of the Visconti family.

It was in 1450, however, that the remarkable Sforza family came to the fore. Muzio Attendolo was the son of a farmer in the Romagna who decided that life held more than the annual round of sowing and reaping. He promptly left home and joined a band of mercenaries. By force of character and success on the battlefield Attendolo rose to the top of his profession and earned the nickname "Sforza," which means "force." Muzio's equally remarkable son Francesco took over as *condottiere* of his father's mercenaries and married the daughter of the Duke of Milan. When the Duke died Francesco had to fight the forces of Venice, Naples, Savoy, Montferrat and Milanese Republicans to enforce his claim to the Ducal throne. Eventually, having enlisted the Medici, Sforza won recognition of his position and established a dynasty which would last until 1535, when Milan fell to the Hapsburgs. Even today the Sforzas are still in evidence, for example Carlo Sforza was Italy's Foreign Minister earlier this century.

Milan stagnated under Hapsburg rule, but in 1706 the city and its lands passed to Austria and the city began to grow larger, richer and more prosperous – a trend which has continued to the present day. There can be little doubt that Milan is the greatest industrial and commercial city in Italy today. Its population of nearly two million accounts for some twelve percent of the nation's economic potential. Industries which predominate include publishing and banking and those producing cars, aeroplanes, electrical equipment, textiles and chemicals. Of all the fine buildings in this prosperous city the two most magnificent are the Cathedral and La Scala. The former was begun in 1386, but work proceeded slowly. The dome was completed around 1500 and the façade in 1809, while the massive bronze doors were not hung until late this century. The rich exterior is decorated with 135 pinnacles and well over 2,000 marble statues. Inside are fifty-two massive pillars topped not by capitals but by a ring of statues. La Scala did not take anywhere near as long to construct. It opened in 1776, having been built by the Empress of Austria, and is now one of the leading half dozen opera houses in the world. Unlike most of the others, La Scala specializes in lesser-known works, though popular works are also presented.

The great cities of northern Italy all lie on the broad lowlands around the River Po. Fertile land and easy communications have led to such a concentration of population in this relatively small area of Italy. To the north, west and east of the lowlands rise the majestic Alps, the snow-capped peaks of which form a boundary between Italy and the rest of Europe. These mountains have long held a fascination for those seeking quiet or adventure. The latter have often taken to climbing, and the Matterhorn is surely one of the finest peaks for such exercise. The 14,691-foot-high mountain straddles Italy's border with Switzerland and remained unconquered until 1865. On July 14th of that year Edward Whymper climbed the peak from the Swiss side and, three days later, a party from Valtournanche scaled the more difficult Italian face.

The Alps, however, are not just famous for mountains; they contain numerous lakes as well. Used by Italians as health and holiday resorts, the lakes are remarkably free of tourism. The largest and probably best known of them is Lake Garda, which has a surface area of 143 square miles. The narrow northern end of the lake belonged to Austria until 1919, when it was surrendered to Italy. The towering cliffs that line the northern shores give way as the lake widens to reveal richly vegetated lands where olives, grapes and citrus fruits grow in abundance. A gentle steamer cruises the lake in summer, offering splendid views of the surroundings. The climate of the lake is warm and mild and is characterized by two winds: the *sover* from the north in the mornings and the *ora* from the south in the afternoons.

Lake Como is similar in many ways, the shore being more mountainous at its north end. It also experiences a similar daily shift in wind direction. Como has an added attraction: it offers excellent fishing for trout and *agoni*, a type of herring.

As well as the scenic beauties of the crystal-clear lakes and the romantic valleys, the Italian Alps have much else to offer the visitor. In recent years areas have been developed as sports centers. These are mainly based in Piedmont and Valle d'Aosta and cater for visitors from all over Europe. Sestriere has more than seventy ski runs available from November to May and many fine hotels. Not all the resorts in Piedmont depend on winter sports; Acqui and St. Vincent are spa towns and the latter has a famous casino.

The lower foothills, away from the commercialized ski runs and the lakes, are as romantic as anybody could wish. Steep-sided valleys are flanked by precipitous hills on which are perched tiny towns. The narrow streets and sheer buildings often date from medieval days when bands of mercenaries led by *condottieri* marched through the valleys. Even today the people have not abandoned their mountain-top towns, though the prospect of climbing the slopes would daunt many. They carry on their lives as if little had changed in the world outside. Little has changed within the towns, with the exception perhaps of a new invention now and then to help with the wine production. Towering above the mountain towns are the scrub-covered peaks where the ruins of a neglected castle can often be found standing in mute testimony to more warlike days.

It is perhaps in northwest Italy that the generally excellent cuisine of the country is at its most delicious. The cheeses of the area are famed throughout the world and include such names as Gorgonzola, Bel Paese, Stracchino and Crescenza. The long, crunchy breadsticks that are served in Italian restaurants around the world originated here, where they are known as *grissini*. Here minestrone is made with special flair and the favorite pasta dish is *agnolotti*, squares stuffed with spinach or cheese. The red wines of the region are probably the best in Italy. Barolo, Sasello and Barbaresco are full-bodied reds which complement the food perfectly. Asti Spumante, their white wine exported internationally, has made a name for itself by successfully undercutting some French champagnes. It was also in this inventive region that, in 1786, a certain A.B. Carpano invented a process of blending wines, herbs and spices to produce vermouth.

Many people cross the border from France, discover the wonderful cuisine, wines and resorts of the northwest and go no further. The rest of Italy, however, has much to offer to both the visitor and resident alike. The magnificent treasures of Italy's past and the vitality of the present create a wonderful atmosphere and a charm which is unique to Italy.

Monte Cervino (previous page and above), 14,691 feet high and known by the Swiss as the Matterhorn, is one of the best-known mountains in the Alps and was first scaled from the steep, terraced Italian side by a group of climbers from the village of Valtournanche, led by the Italian guide Giovanni Antonio Carrel. However, it was conquered for the first time ever three days before that climb from the less severe Swiss side by the British artist and climber Edward Whymper, who lost four colleagues in the descent, leaving only himself and two guides as survivors. Right: mountain water courses past Monte Breuil-Cervina in the Valle d'Aosta (these pages), northwest Italy. The Valle d'Aosta is a long, deep furrow between Europe's highest mountains formed by the Dora Báltea River and its tributaries. Overleaf: the Dolomites from Pordoi Pass (Passo Pordoi); at 7,536 feet it is the highest pass in the mountains.

Below: the peaks of the Dolomites (these pages). Facing page: Passo Tre Croci, not far from the lake town of Misurina. Overleaf: Livigno.

Left: Cortina d'Ampezzo, capital of Venetia's Dolomite Mountains. This town, one of Italy's most popular centers for winter sports, hosted the Winter Olympics in 1956. Overleaf: Langkofel, Dolomites.

Milan (Milano) is the thriving capital of Lombardy, a region that extends from the central Alps to the Po Valley. It is Italy's second-largest city after Rome, and is the country's commercial capital and principal industrial center, housing one of the largest silk markets in Europe. Henry James, while commenting on the "delight of seeing the North melt slowly into the South," said also that Milan was more "the last of the prose capitals than the first of the poetic." But Mark Twain seems to have disagreed when he described the Duomo, or Cathedral (right), as "a poem in marble." D.H. Lawrence was not similarly inclined toward the Duomo, however, and described it as "an imitation hedgehog of a cathedral." This Duomo, the largest Gothic building in Italy, was begun under the orders of Gian Galeazzo Visconti in 1386 and construction continued throughout the centuries under a variety of European masters. It was eventually consecrated in 1577 and the façade was finally finished in 1809, under the orders of Napoleon. Its overall design was the work of another Frenchman, Nicolas de Bonaventure, and of a Modenese architect, Filippino degli Organi.

Above: Lago d'Idro. Top: the Arch of Peace (Arco di Pace) in Milan. The restored, thirteenth-century castle of the Scaligers, called Rocca Scaligera (right), dominates Sirmione on Lago di Garda. The castle, jutting out into the lake on a peninsula, was the Scaliger stronghold. The family ruled Verona. Dante is said to have stayed here while he was in political exile from Florence, protected by Cangrande I, the greatest Scaliger. It was also to this beautiful town, then called Sirmio, that the Roman poet Catullus retreated to heal the emotional scars of an intense and unhappy love affair with a married patrician whom, in his twenty-five poems about her, he called Lesbia. "What joy is like it? to be quit of care | And drop my load, and after weary miles | Come home, and sink upon the bed that so | I used to dream of: this one thing is worth | All that long service. Hail sweet Sirmio! | Welcome thy lord with laughter and give back | Your laughter, waters of the Lydian lake: | Laugh, home of mine, with all your maddest mirth."

Left and below: Lago di Garda, the largest lake in Italy's lake district. To the north it is sheltered by the lofty Dolomites, and to the east by the mountain chain of Monte Baldo. Bottom: Verona's first-century-AD Roman amphitheater, called the Arena. This huge amphitheater can seat up to 25,000 spectators, and so good are its acoustics that operas are still staged there during the summer months and all the audience, however high up they are, can hear. The Arena was built from flint, brick and the distinctive pink marble of the Veneto region, giving it the rosy tinge characteristic of Verona. Verona is famous for many things – great architects, families and painters such as Veronese and Pisano – but perhaps it will never be more famous for anything than it is for a certain pair of "star-cross'd lovers" celebrated immortally by Shakespeare: "That while Verona by that name is known, | There shall no figure at such rate be set | As that of true and faithful Juliet … For never was a story of more woe | Than this of Juliet and her Romeo." Overleaf: Lazise harbor on Lago di Garda.

By 1817, when Byron visited Venice (Venezia) (these pages), "la Serenissima, Queen of the Adriatic" was already in decline. However, during the first half of the fifteenth century, Venice was at the peak of her power as the mighty city of commerce where East met West and the sea met the sky. The sea was Venice's fortune. Pope Alexander III gave the Doge a ring, in return for his military support, signifying Venetian maritime ascendancy. Each Ascension Day, from 1173 to 1797, the Doge would sail out to San Nicolò and cast a replica of the Pope's ring into the water, saying "We wed thee, Sea, in token of our perpetual rule." However, with the fall of Constantinople to the Turks in 1453 and the trade possibilities opened up by the discovery of America in 1492, the decline of Venice began, culminating in Napoleon's invasion in 1797. Despite the decline of Venice, visitors and writers such as Byron have loved her, perhaps for the very precariousness of her state perched as she is on over one hundred sinking islands and barely able to resist the importunity of her traditional husband, the sea. Above: Franchetti Palace on the Grand Canal (Canal Grande). Left and top: the white domes of Santa Maria della Salute. Known simply as the Salute, this church was built by Baldassare Longhena between 1631 and 1681 as a symbol of hope and in fulfilment of a vow following the devastation of a year of plague. Henry James described the Salute as being "like some great lady on the threshold of her saloon … with her domes and scrolls, her scalloped buttresses and statues forming a pompous crown, and her wide steps disposed on the ground like the train of a robe." This grand church contains paintings by Titian, Tintoretto and Giordano.

Venetian gondoliers (these pages) are well known for their propensity to sing. So much so that Verdi refused to allow the tenor or the orchestra to have the music for La Donna e Mobile *from his opera* Rigoletto *until just before its opening night in Venice, in order to prevent the gondoliers from learning of it and singing it to their customers before the première, thereby spoiling its impact. Verdi was right in assuming gondoliers would love this song; they still sing it to visitors as they ferry them past the sights.*

Above: the Palazzo Ducale, a "vast and sumptuous pile" in the words of Byron. So grand was its Grand Council Chamber, and so lavish the hospitality experienced there that Henri II of France pronounced that "if I were not King of France, I would like to be a citizen of Venice." Top: the gilded and enamelled clockface of the Clock Tower (Torre dell' Orologio), built by Coducci on the Piazza San Marco in 1496. The dial bears the signs of the zodiac, and on its summit two bronze jacks strike the hour on the great bell. They have done so now for over 500 years. On feast days three Magi, preceded by a herald, move bowing around the statue of the Virgin. It is thought that Mauro Codussi designed the tower. Pietro Lombardo added its two wings. Before the Clock Tower are the massive horses which adorn a platform on the front of St. Mark's Basilica (Basilica San Marco). These Greco-Roman bronzes were brought from Constantinople by Doge Dandolo in 1204. Napoleon later relocated them, and they remained in Paris until his fall. They have been replaced with copies recently and the originals, safe from the effects of the weather, are housed in the Basilica's museum. Right: Piazzetta San Marco. Its two famous cafés, Florian and Quadri, have entertained tourists throughout the years. Illustrious coffee drinkers of the past have included writers and poets Henry James, Marcel Proust, Evelyn Waugh, Ernest Hemingway, the Brownings, Shelley and Byron – to name but a few.

Above: the Campanile and the Palazzo Ducale. Facing page: the Salute. The regatta (overleaf) on the Grand Canal is the result of a 700-year-old tradition going back, it is thought, to a pursuit of raiders abducting Venetian women. Today's display reenacts a later event, the ornate welcome given by Venice to the Queen of Cyprus when she visited the city in 1489. Either way, Venice puts on her fifteenth-century finery and launches her opulent bissone (barges), resplendent with the heraldic crests of noble Venetian families, to celebrate their respect for a woman. Small wonder that Charles V chose Italian for the fair sex when he said: "to God I speak Spanish, to women Italian, to men French, and to my horse – German."

Below: a view from the Rialto Bridge. The Bridge of Sighs (Ponte dei Sospiri) (right) links the east wing of the Palazzo Ducale to the New Prisons over Rio di Palazzo. The bridge was named for the prisoners who glimpsed their last of the world through its dense, stone latticework on their way to death or imprisonment and heaved a sigh. Perhaps the most famous "guest" of the Doge to cross it was Casanova, convicted in 1755 as a magician. He didn't sigh for long but made a spectacular escape on October 31, 1756. Below right: a narrow canal behind Piazza San Marco.

Left: the tilted bell tower of Longhena's church, San Giorgio dei Greci, built circa 1678. Above left: a bridge on Calle de la Stua. Above: a private gondola park near the Rialto on the Grand Canal. Overleaf: the golden ball of the Punta della Dogana, the old Custom House, near the Salute.

Above: Portofino harbor. Portofino was once a tiny, beautiful fishing village, but it was discovered after the Second World War by the jet set and now, where once only fishing boats bobbed, row upon row of expensive yachts are moored. Facing page: the green-shuttered houses of Riomaggiore, Liguria (these pages and overleaf), leaning into the steep, stratified slope. Overleaf: the fishing village of Portovenere.

Facing page: Diano Marina, a busy beach resort on the Ponente Riviera, Liguria (these pages and overleaf). Above: the harbor and medieval castle of the old Pisan village of Lerici, on the eastern shore of the Gulf of La Spezia, near where the poet Shelley rented a house in 1822. Lord Byron swam all the way from Portovenere across the Gulf to visit Shelley there – a trip that takes twenty minutes by boat. Shelley had less luck with the Gulf's waters: he drowned returning from Leghorn by boat. A plaque in Casa Magni commemorates him in lush Italian, which translates as: "Sailing on a fragile bark he was landed by an unforeseen chance to the silence of the Elisean Fields." The Gulf of La Spezia was beloved of so many poets, among them Dante and Petrach, that it is often called simply Golfo dei Poeti. Overleaf: Rapallo.

The shifting Tuscan subsoil which caused Bonanno Pisano's Leaning Tower (facing page) to tilt as it was being built between 1173 and 1350 was not the only hazard afforded by the tower to the good citizens of Pisa (these pages). Pisan-born astronomer and physicist, Galileo, is said to have utilized its tilt to drop weights from its top – thereby investigating the nature of gravity and disproving Aristotle's theories of acceleration. The neighboring Duomo (above) also aided the advancement of science. A swinging lamp there led Galileo to formulate the pendulum theory. But the Church ceased to inspire him when he fell foul of the Inquisition in 1616 over his support for Copernicanism.

Florence (Firenze) was once the capital of Tuscany and the cradle of the Renaissance. Indeed, the archetypical Renaissance man, Leonardo da Vinci, was born just outside this city, known aptly as "La Bella." The Renaissance was heralded by a series of public work commissions. One of them was issued as a competition to determine who would design and build the dome for the Duomo, or Cathedral of Santa Maria del Fiore (right). Brunelleschi won it and, in 1420, began to construct the first massive dome since Ancient times. The finished structure inspired Michelangelo to produce the dome on St. Peter's in Rome. Dante was born only a few streets away from the Duomo. He was exiled from Florence in 1302, before Brunelleschi began his dome, but he would have seen some of the building as work had started on the body of the Duomo in 1296 under the direction of sculptor and architect Arnolfo di Cambio; it continued until 1436. The Duomo's slender neighbor, the Campanile, was begun in 1334 by Giotto, and is faced with bas-reliefs and panels of different colored marbles – red from Siena, white from Carrara, and green from Prato. Pisano took over when Giotto died three years after work started, and Francesco Talenti took over after him. Both Talenti and Pisano stuck to Giotto's design with the exception of not adding a ninety-eight-foot tower Giotto had planned. Overleaf: a view of Florence from the Cathedral.

Michelangelo's statue of David (above), begun in 1501 and completed in 1504, now stands in Florence's Galleria dell'Accademia. The new Republic of Florence commissioned the statue as an allegory of the moral strength of the city, and it was carved from a huge block of marble reserved for the purpose since 1462. The marble was imperfect, Michelangelo called it "spoilt," and yet David, dating from the master's "juvenile period," is considered to be one of the finest humanist renditions of man in his heroic state. The sculpture originally stood before the Palazzo Vecchio in Piazza della Signoria, but was taken into the gallery in 1882 as a safety measure and set up in an apse designed especially for it by architect De Fabris. Right: the 1576 Neptune Fountain by Ammannati in the Piazza della Signoria.

Left: the Ponte Vecchio, Florence (these pages). This, Florence's oldest bridge, has been rebuilt several times, and crosses the River Arno at its narrowest point. Since 1593 it has been lined with jewelers' shops. Above: the Duomo and the octagonal, Romanesque Baptistry of San Giovanni, dating from the ninth century. The Baptistry became the subject of a competition in 1401 for the design of its north doors, won by Ghiberti from Brunelleschi. Its east doors, also the work of Ghiberti, were dubbed "the gates of Paradise" by Michelangelo, so magnificent are they. Top: the Piazza della Signoria before the thirteenth-century Palazzo Vecchio with its splendid bell tower by Arnolfo di Cambio. Architecture like this spurred Fanny Burney to write "Traveling is the ruin of all happiness! There's no looking at a building here after seeing Italy." The famous art gallery, Galleria degli Uffizi, also faces onto this square in the middle of which a circular slab marks the spot where the reformer monk Savonarola was hanged and burned in 1498 for heresy – in the very square where he had enacted the "burning of the vanities," a destruction by fire of lewd pictures, gambling tables, jewelry, etcetera, a year earlier.

The Duomo (these pages) of Siena (these pages and overleaf), initially modeled on Orvieto Cathedral, was begun by Giovanni Pisano in 1229; its façade of red, black and white marble was finally completed in 1380, though the highly ornate carvings and mosaics date from a restoration in the nineteenth century. The dignified, Romanesque campanile beside it was begun in 1313. Overleaf: the shell-shaped Piazza del Campo before the Palazzo Pubblico, or Town Hall, which was Siena's seat of government. The slender Torre del Mangia, which rises from one side of the Palazzo's exterior, was designed by Lippo Memmi. It was named mangia (wastrel) after one of its fondly remembered bellringers. The Piazza is divided into nine segments by white lines radiating from the Palazzo outward, to symbolize the historical governing Council of Nine "Good Men." It is also where Siena's famous Palio horse race takes place.

Facing page: a Gothic-style church in the hills near Spoleto seems to lift the green canopy of the trees up into its roof. St. Francis said that he had never seen anything so pleasing as the Spoleto Valley. He may have been a little less pleased by some of the local inhabitants. Spoleto was once the home of Lucretia Borgia, infamous daughter of Pope Alexander VI and probably mother of his child. Above: the hilltop town of Trevi, Umbria.

These pages: the "Eternal City" of Rome (Roma). Above: the Palazzo del Senatore, or the Senate, part of the Capitol complex on Monte Capitolino. The Senate is the official residence of the Mayor of Rome. At the top of the steps leading to it stand the statues of Castor and Pollux, the Heavenly Twins – known as the Dioscuri. The steps and the Capitol were designed by Michelangelo during the sixteenth century. The Palazzo del Senatore is a twelfth-century building which was reworked between 1582 and 1602. Top: the Trevi Fountain off the Via delle Muratte. Right: the Castel Sant' Angelo and the Basilica of St. Peter beyond the River Tiber. The Castel is the site where Puccini chose to have Act III of his opera Tosca performed. Act I is performed in the ornate Baroque church of S. Andrea della Valle, and Act II is staged across the Tiber in the Palazzo Farnese – a magnificent Renaissance palace. Castel Sant' Angelo, Hadrian's mausoleum, was begun by him in AD 135 and was finished by Antoninus Pius six years later. It became a fortress and later a prison. The huge bronze angel on the parapet, the spot from which Tosca throws herself to her death at the end of the opera, stands on top of a chapel that Gregory the Great had built there during the sixth century to mark the apparition of an angel during the plague of AD 590. The angel was seen sheathing his sword, which the Pope saw as a sign that the plague was over. Ponte Sant' Angelo, linking the Castel to the left bank of the Tiber, is decorated with angels carved by Bernini, and with statues of saints Peter and Paul.

The Vittoriano, or the National Monument to Victor Emmanuel II, Rome. Completed in 1911 on the Capitoline Hill, this neoclassical monument celebrates the first king of a unified Italy after 1,400 years of national fragmentation. He achieved national unification partly through giving the great Italian statesman Cavour scope to exercise his diplomatic efforts on Italy's behalf, thus building up the country's credibility as an independent state. Moreover, after Cavour's death, the King acquired Venetia and Rome. He also encouraged Garibaldi to conquer Sicily and Naples, then marched to meet him at Rome, risking excommunication from Pope Pius IX. Pius eventually forgave Victor Emmanuel for invading Papal territory, recognizing that his vision of Rome as Italy's natural capital was right, and allowed the King to be buried in the Pantheon. Locals tend to dislike his monument however, referring to it as the "Typewriter" or the "Wedding Cake."

Above: the Fountain of Neptune, and (facing page) the Fountain of Moors, both found in the seventeenth-century Piazza Navona, Rome (these pages). The Fountain of the Moors is a work by Bernini while, opposite it, the Fountain of Neptune – whose full title translates magnificently as Neptune Wrestling With a Marine Monster, Sea Horses and Nereids – is the work of Della Bitta and Zappalà.

The Arco di Settimio Severo, or Triple Arch of Septimus Severus (right), has survived almost intact among the ruins of the Roman Forum (these pages). Behind it can be seen the Palazzo del Senatore and the white, Brescia-marble National Monument to Victor Emmanuel II. This arch was built in AD 203 to honor the victories won by its eponymous emperor and his sons Caracalla and Geta over the Parthians. The Arco di Tito, or the Arch of Titus (bottom), stands at the base of the Clivus Palatinus beyond the ruined temples of Vespasianus (Titus' father) and Castor and Pollux. It was erected in AD 81 to commemorate the capture of Jerusalem by Titus in AD 70. But when Titus, the "darling of the human race" according to Suetonius, captured Jerusalem he set in motion the great Diaspora, or scattering, of the Jews whom he exiled from Babylon. It is thought that one million Jews died during this campaign. To this day many devout Jews refuse to pass under the arch.

The Trevi Fountain, Rome. The building of this spectacular fountain was ordered by Pope Clement XII and Salvi, the sculptor, finished it in 1762 following designs by Bernini. It benefits from having the Palazzo Poli as a background. The centerpiece shows Neptune, god of the sea, being hauled in his chariot by two large tritons. He is flanked by figures representing Health and Fertility. Legend holds that whoever tosses a coin backward, over his or her head, into the fountain will one day return to throw in another.

Top: Bernini's vast Colonnade, enclosing St. Peter's Square (right), in the Vatican City. The square took him eleven years to complete, beginning in 1656. In the center of this vast area stands an obelisk dating from the first century BC. It came originally from Heliopolis in Egypt to Rome in AD 37, by order of Caligula. Sixtus V had it placed in its present position in 1585 and at the top of it rests a relic of the Holy Cross. Bernini's square has held upward of 400,000 people at one time. The Vatican City covers just 109 acres, but it wasn't always so small. It began as a gift of Papal States from Pepin the Short to Pope Stephen II during the eighth century. The Papal States were lost in 1870, however, when Italy was unified with Rome as its capital. The Lateran Treaty of 1929 reestablished the territory as an independent state, but in 1970 Pope Paul VI disbanded the Vatican army, retaining only the splendidly colorful Swiss Guard who protect it to this day. Their uniforms were designed by Michelangelo in the colors of the Medici popes: red, yellow and blue. The Guard comprises young, unmarried, Catholic Swiss men between the ages of nineteen and twenty-five. Although small in area, the Vatican issues its own money and has its own post office, radio station, observatory and power station. Above: the National Monument to Victor Emmanuel II.

Basilica di San Pietro, known the world over as St. Peter's, in the Vatican City. The first church on this site was consecrated in AD 326, built at the behest of Pope Sylvester by Constantine the Great. The present building was begun by Pope Julius II in 1506. He commissioned Bramante to design it. When Bramante died, in 1514, Raphael took over. Eventually, in 1547, Michelangelo took charge. Its dome was his last work – placing it onto the church largely built by his old rival, Bramante, occupied his old age. The difficult, quick-tempered and querulous master had been much troubled about the nature of his art. In some of his poems he debated soberly whether or not it had been sinful and he was obviously sincere in his doubts as he refused payment for this huge cupola, regarding it as a work dedicated to the greater glory of God which he preferred not to be sullied by worldly gain. Pope Julius II first called Michelangelo to Rome from Florence in 1496 to carve his tomb. The artist became so famous and was so prolific during his lifetime that it is not surprising that Mark Twain wrote in near exasperation, "Enough! Say no more! Lump the whole thing! Say that the Creator made Italy from designs by Michael Angelo!"

These pages: the Colosseum, Rome, originally the Flavian Amphitheater, and begun by Vespasian in
AD 75. Above: the substructures beneath the Colosseum's arena. This great building was erected over the
lake of Nero's Domus Aurea, or Golden House. It is thought that Vespasian drained the lake and had a
public monument constructed in its place as a sign that the profligate days of Nero were over. Vespasian's
son Titus, raised the amphitheater to four storeys, inaugurating it in AD 80 with 100 days of gladiatorial
contests which involved 1,000 gladiators and 5,000 wild animals. It held 45,000 spectators. The
Colosseum's extensive substructures housed hoists, stage props, machinery and cages for the wild beasts
that were to fight to the death in the arena. The arena could also be flooded to stage grand-scale, mock
naval battles. Honorius banned the brutal gladiatorial contests in AD 404. Eventually Pope Benedict XIV
consecrated the ruins in respect for all the Christians who had been martyred there. The structure had
suffered from being used as a fortress by Roman nobles and from the effects of earthquakes during the
Middle Ages.

Below and below right: the Spanish Steps, leading from the Piazza di Spagna to the Church of Trinità dei Monti, Rome (these pages). The steps were designed and built by architects de Sanctis and Specchi during the eighteenth century. At the foot of these steps lies the Keats-Shelley Memorial House, in which the poet Keats died in 1821. The area received its name during the seventeenth century when the Spanish Embassy moved to Piazza di Spagna. Right: the Via Veneto. This road was once the fashionable focus of Rome's Dolce Vita, or good life, and still is today though some of its glamour has faded. Many of Rome's finest hotels are found here.

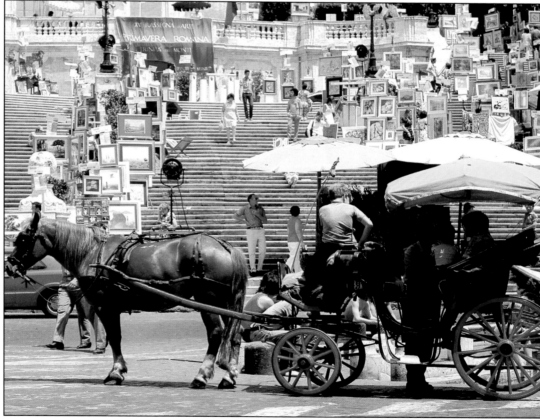

Bottom: St. Peter's, Rome (these pages). Left: the three Corinthian columns of the Temple of Vespasian (Tempio di Vespasiano), dating from the first century AD. When Vespasian died it is reported that his last words were Vae, puto deus fio, "Oh dear, I think I am becoming a god." Upon his death he was promptly deified. Across the road from the Temple of Vespasian stand the eight, fourth-century Ionic columns of the Temple of Saturn (Tempio di Saturno) in the Roman Forum. The Temple of Saturn was begun in the sixth century BC, making it one of the oldest temples still partly standing. Below: a corner of the Temple of Saturn and beyond it the three remaining columns of the Temple of Castor and Pollux (Tempio di Castore e Polluce) in the Forum. The low ruins behind the Temple of Castor and Pollux are the remains of the House of the Vestal Virgins (Casa delle Vestali). Vesta was the Roman goddess of the hearth and in her temple six virgins took turns to tend her sacred flame. Should they neglect their duty in this respect they were scourged by the priest. A vestal virgin served for thirty years, beginning at the age of six. During this time a rule of chastity was imposed. When the thirty years were up, vestals were allowed to marry – but many chose not to, believing it to be unlucky. For errant vestal virgins the Emperor Domitian instituted burial alive as a punishment for the girl, while her lover was stoned to death.

*Facing page: the Temple of Genii Augusti, and (above) tombs in the Necropoli, or cemetery,
outside Pompeii (these pages).*

Above: a steep street in Capri town. Right: the twelfth-century Tower of Damecuta, on Capri's northwest coast. In AD 27, the Emperor Tiberius retired to Capri, which was known as the Island of Goats, probably because it was felt that no other type of beast could scale the island's precipitous heights. However, Tiberius developed something of a reputation on Capri, summed up by Suetonius who wrote that the Emperor "devised little nooks of lechery in the woods and glades … and had boys and girls dressed up as pans and nymphs posted in front of caverns or grottoes; so that the island was now openly and generally called 'Caprineum,' because of his goatish antics." Overleaf: Porto Sannazzaro, the picturesque harbor of Mergellina, a suburb of Naples.

Below: the Marina Grande, Capri, and (right) bathers in Sorrento harbor (below right). Sorrento, surrounded by orange and lemon groves, lies on the south side of the Bay of Naples. This town was the birthplace of the famous Renaissance poet Tasso in 1544, and here, in 1867, Ibsen finished **Peer Gynt***. Eleven years later, it was in Sorrento that Wagner and Neitzsche quarreled about their divergent philosophies and parted. Today Sorrento is chiefly known for being a charming resort town.*

These pages: the stepped, Moorish houses of Positano, once a fishing village, now a tourist center. Overleaf: the church and tenth-century fishing port of Atrani on the rocky south coast of the Sorrento peninsula, called Costiera Amalfitana.

Above: the Gulf of Salerno seen from the gardens of Palazzo Rufolo in Ravello. Facing page: the village of Rivello in the arid mountains above the Gulf of Policastro.

Top: the Temple of Concord (Tempio della Concordia), and (above) the Temple of Castor and Pollux (Tempio di Castore e Polluce) in Agrigento, Sicily (these pages). The town was founded around 581 BC by Greek colonists from Gela. When the Greek poet Pindar visited Agrigento he described it as "the fairest city of mortal men." The Temple of Concord, converted into a church in AD 597, still has thirty-four columns standing and is one of the world's best-preserved Ancient temples. The four columns of the Temple of Castor and Pollux were re-erected. Right: a Doric temple, known to archaeologists as Temple E, on the Acropolis at Selinunte. The town was founded as Selinous in 651 or 628 BC by Greek colonists who named it for the wild celery (selinon in Greek) they found growing there. Many of the town's fine Doric temples, which are still being excavated, collapsed during violent earthquakes throughout the fifth to eighth centuries AD.

Above: the beach resort of Mondello, near Palermo. Facing page: Taormina, high on a terrace above the Ionian Sea. Overleaf: dangerous, beautiful Mount Etna, Sicily. D.H. Lawrence described this deceptive volcano as "This timeless Grecian Etna, in her lower-heaven loveliness, so lovely, so lovely, what a torturer! … How many men, how many races, has Etna put to flight? It was she who broke the quick of the Greek soul. And after the Greeks, she gave the Romans, the Normans, the Arabs, the Spaniards, the French, the Italians, even the English, she have them all their inspired hour and broke their souls."

INDEX